MASTERING THE ART OF
Interviewing

MASTERING THE ART OF
Interviewing

A Guide To Successful Interviewing

BRIAN L.
BURNS

outskirtspress
DENVER, COLORADO

Outskirts Press, Inc.
http://www.outskirtspress.com

ISBN: 978-1-4787-5713-9

Outskirts Press and the "OP" logo are trademarks belonging to Outskirts Press, Inc.

PRINTED IN THE UNITED STATES OF AMERICA

This book is dedicated to:

All of the men and women, in the Armed Forces and my fellow veterans. Thank you and I love you all! All of the men and women with college degrees and the men and women without college degrees. The ones that was laid off after 18+ years and the ones that was laid off after 3 months due to the economy. The ones that pound the pavement everyday literally or via the web searching for that next paying job so they can feed their families. This book is to you because honest hard working people such as yourselves are the backbone of this country.

Table of Contents

ACKNOWLEDGEMENTS ix

INTRODUCTION... 1

DO YOUR RESEARCH 5

UPDATE YOUR RESUME 10

THE SCREENING PROCESS... 12

WHAT SHOULD I TAKE?... 14

PERSONAL PRESENTATION 21

LOCATION AWARENESS 31

THE ARRIVAL 33

THE ACTUAL INTERVIEW 35

NOW IT'S TIME TO TALK.. 42

RESPONDING TO DIFFICULT QUESTIONS 49

QUESTIONS THE INTERVIEWER SHOULD BE ASKED 55

HAVE A NICE DAY. THE FOLLOW-UP 57

CONCLUSION 59

SOCIAL NETWORKING (Appendix A) 60

INTERVIEWING CHECKLIST (Appendix B) 64

LIST OF QUESTIONS (APPENDIX C) 67

BIBLIOGRAPHY 78

ACKNOWLEDGEMENTS

First, I want to thank God for my existence. If it wasn't for him, I would not be here.

To my parents,(all three of them), Mr. & Mrs. Melvin and Diane Griffin and Mr. Charles Burns, thank you for teaching me how to be a God fearing man and that whatever I strived for, I can accomplish.

To my children, Bra'zhelle, Brian II, Brianca and Brittney, thank you for giving me the inspiration to strive for more. If I want you to strive to fulfill your true potential, then I must set the example.

To my grandmother, Mrs. Melvina "Malo" Russell, who is the matriarch of my family. You always supported me without judgment and was always there when I needed it and was not always willing to ask for it. I thank you.

To my mentors, Cassandra Lee and Sporty King, thank you for always being real with me and showing me the things that I need to and need not do in order to move forward to make my dreams a reality.

To Todd and Theresa Banks, my brother and sister from another mother, thank you for guiding me through this process. This was truly a journey and I couldn't have done it without you.

To Fruenze Deadmon Sr., thank you for being someone that I can talk to when things got really tough and for you keeping it real even when sometimes I didn't want to see reality. Thanks Bro.

To Lorrie Walker, thank you for being my prayer partner and keeping me focused on God. Always reminding me that Philippians 4:13 states: "I can do all things through Christ which strengthens me." And to remember Psalms 121:1: "I will lift up mine eyes unto the hills, from whence cometh my help. My help cometh from the LORD." Thank you for being the words of spiritual encouragement.

To Mrs. Carol Gearring, you were the first to believe in my writing and encouraged me to write at an early age. You always believed in me and my potential. For that I truly want to thank you.

To Ken Calvin, thank you for your words of encouragement every time you saw me. You let me know how much I can accomplish and always have had my back personally and professionally.

To Abdul Mahdi, thank you for the information and resources.

To Nina Sinclair Burns, thank you for inspiring me to continue to write.

INTRODUCTION

Richard, a professional of fifteen years, has been out of work for two years now. He has submitted many applications and resumes. The mortgage is due and his unemployment benefits have expired. Richard believes that there must be a job out there for a professional with his experience. The telephone rings and he finally gets the break he was hoping for. A company asked Richard in for an interview. Finally, a company invites Richard to interview for a position that matched his skills.

Thomas is a blue collar worker who has been out of work for three years. He doesn't have a college degree but is very skilled at what he does. Thomas has done odd jobs to supplement his unemployment benefits which ended a year ago. Thomas has submitted applications and resumes to various companies since his lay off. Thomas finally got an interview from one company he has always wanted to work for.

Billy is a sixteen year old high school student that saw the car of his dreams. He knows that he must get a job in order to purchase the car that he wants. Excited about the prospect of getting a car, Billy submitted applications via internet and everywhere he saw a help wanted sign displayed. Anxiously awaiting the telephone to ring from anyone, he continued to submit applications via the internet. The telephone rang and Billy finally got his first interview.

OUT WITH THE OLD

In today's economy, the above situations are very common. This may not have been true twenty five years ago. With the massive layoffs, the unemployment rate has fluctuated. Today's job market is extremely competitive. The economy is slowly recovering and many companies are looking to fill vacancies with the most qualified applicants. There are an extremely high number of qualified personnel looking for employment than ever before.

Many qualified individuals have gone through the interview process only to lose the job to less qualified applicants. Why? If they were the most qualified, then why wouldn't they get the job? They have relied on an older interviewing process. The interviewing process from twenty to twenty-five years ago, (better known as the traditional interviewing process), is no longer solely used. This interviewing process has evolved.

In "Traditional Interviews", the questions that are asked typically will have a straight forward answer. The employer was mostly concerned about these things.

1. Can you do the job?

2. Where do you see yourself in 5 years?

3. Can you get to work on time?

4. How much are you expecting to get paid?

There are a few more questions, such as *"What are your strengths and weaknesses?"* or *"What major challenges have you faced in your career?"*

but those stated are the main questions an employer wanted to know in a traditional interview.

IN WITH THE NEW

In recent years, the interviewing process has evolved into what is now known as ***Situational Interviews*** or ***Behavioral Interviews.*** Although referred to by two different names, the interviewing process is the same.

What is a Behavioral/Situational interview? Behavioral/Situational based interviewing is interviewing based on discovering how you (the applicant) behave in specific employment-related situations. The logic for this type of interviewing is to see how you behaved in the past, in which this will predict how you will behave in the future (i.e. past performance predicts future performance).

A major mistake that most applicants make when they receive that invitation for an interview is that they do not properly prepare themselves. A surgeon cannot perform surgery without being properly prepared. First of all, he must have the proper training, the right certifications and licenses plus have the proper equipment to perform the surgery successfully. Not only must an applicant understand the interviewing process but they must also properly prepare for the interview. Preparation starts long before the first question is asked at the actual interview.

There are several different types of interviews such as *telephone interviews, task-oriented interviews, team interviews, board or panel interviews, etc.* The Behavioral Interview will be the focus in this guide. This guide is designed to help you properly prepare for the interview from the time you receive the call inviting you to participate in an interview, to the thank you correspondence to the company after the interview. These simple things will help you stand out in the actual interview. This guide will give you a competitive advantage of getting that job. Be prepared to adapt to both styles.

DO YOUR RESEARCH

Before applying, do your research. Your cover letter should reflect some knowledge of the company (i.e. matching your skills to the job description and incorporating a recently awarded accomplishment of the company). Often times many applicants enter into an interview without having the knowledge of what that company actually does. They also do not know the history of the company, what direction the company is heading or the awards the company has received. Not knowing this information could be the downfall of the interview. The best thing to do is *"DO YOUR RESEARCH."*

Luckily there are diverse resources, many of them free or cheap and available on the Internet. This will enable you to achieve that competitive edge if you're willing to do the research needed to differentiate yourself from other applicants.

Sources

The company's website is one of the best places to get the information that is needed. Trade Journals (i.e such as ProQuest), news sources (i.e NewsLink, Refdesk or bizjournals.com), and links such as Hoover's Online are additional valuable sources to get vital information that is beneficial to know for the interview.

When doing your research, use the company's website and other resources to gain information on the following:

Know the Company's Vision and Mission Statements.-Compatibility

The Vision/Mission statements are often clearly posted. The vision statement gives the "vision" of the company. This tells what goal a company wants to ultimately achieve. The mission statement is a road map on how a company will achieve that goal. Knowing these two statements verbatim will not only help you better understand what a company does, but they will help you see the bigger picture of the company.

Know the Company's History.- Longevity; Stability vs Organization Turnover

The history is the very foundation of a company. Knowing who started the company and what year the company was founded is a must. Was there a proprietorship, partners or was it an expansion from a larger company? How long did it take to expand? Were there any financial difficulties in the beginning? Often time, in chronological order, the history states the events leading up to why a company is where it is presently. Gathering as much information as possible will increase your chances of wowing the interviewer.

Always find the listing of awards.-Level of Excellence

Awards show the accomplishments of a company. What are the most recent awards and what was it for? Which awards were received more than once? What are the most prestigious awards the company has received to date? All awards and honors are important. Therefore, having a vast knowledge of this area will help you understand the level of excellence the company pursues.

Research press releases so that you can know what is going on in the company.

When doing your research, be sure to review the company's press releases. The company may be merging or expanding into a new location or a new product line. A press release can give you an indication of the types of charities in which a company supports. A press release will give you a quick glimpse of valuable, public information about the company that can come in handy for your interview.

Find out what charities the company supports.

Some companies are major contributors to charities. Do they participate or sponsor cancer walks? Do they host events for a HIV/AIDS foundation? Do they participate in March of Dimes or other children's charities? Whether or not the company encourages employees to participate is a wealth of information. This shows the level of commitment a company expects its employees to have for a particular charity. Find out what is the next charitable event and participate in it. This will not only impress the interviewer but it will show that you care about others and their wellbeing and are willing to go above and beyond what the job requires. *Mention the charities at the formal interview only if charity interests you.

Know what product or service the company is offering.

Throughout my research, many hiring managers expressed to me that some applicants are not aware of the products and services the company that they are interviewing for offers. It seems as though if an applicant applies for a position, then they would know what products and services the company has to offer. This seems like a no brainer, right? Unfortunately, it is not as obvious as it seems. Merrill Lynch does not just offer general investment accounts, but they also offer retirement accounts for individuals. Merrill Lynch offers a wide variety of business accounts, in addition to the individual investment accounts. This is the reason why it is important to know the products and services of the company that you are applying. Besides, not knowing this information is definitely a deal breaker.

Have a general idea of the industry and know the company's competitors.

This is helpful information. Knowing the trends of the industry will give you a better understanding of the company's position in the industry and its competitors. By understanding Wal-Mart's competitors such as Target and Kohls, gives you an advantage. You will be able to answer company related questions in more detail such as: *"I believe that I can be an asset to the company because I am dedicated to doing cutting edge research. I noticed that there is a trend of teens wearing skinny jeans in the southwest region. Your competitors have not noticed this up and coming trend in that region as of yet."* This will impress the hiring manager because you not only have done your research but also may have brought something to his attention that could benefit the company.

Know and understand the job description.

Many applicants enter an interview with either a vague understanding or misunderstanding of the job description or the job requirements. Make sure you understand fully what the job description states. It is not wise to apply for a position just because it requires the degree that you possess. When a hiring manager asks you in for an interview and you have applied for various positions in that particular company, ask him/her at that time which position you are interviewing for if it is not already stated. It is embarrassing to enter into an interview prepared to answer questions for one position and realize during the interview that you are there for another position.

UPDATE YOUR RESUME

Review and revise your resume.

Look over your resume and make sure the latest information is on there (i.e. education, job history). Have someone else read your resume in order to identify anything that you may have missed. If possible, get someone that is proficient in resume writing to read your resume. Then, read through your resume again. Look for any typos that may have been missed by the person that read it for you.

Know what's on your resume.

It is very important to know what is on your resume. Several hiring managers expressed concern about candidates not knowing what is on their own resume. How embarrassing would it be if the interviewer asks you a question about what is on your resume and the look on your face is that of a clueless person? Having to be reminded of what is on your resume by the interviewer is not a good sign. It may also bring your integrity into question. That is something that you don't want to happen because that is definitely a deal breaker.

Make sure your resume is fact not fiction.

"Last year I took a one day crash course on a particular software application. Since that day I have not used the software. Can I put it on my resume that I am proficient with that software?

It is very important that you do not embellish on your resume. We all would like to do this on our resumes to give us a competitive advantage. Embellishing on your resume could be proven detrimental to you. If found out that you put something on your resume that is not true, then not getting the job will not be the worst thing that could possibly happen. Your integrity could be in question. If this happens, then your career may have ended before it began. Remember, in any industry, everyone knows everyone else. If you interview with a company and your integrity is in question, the hiring manager or the interviewer may know the person that calls you in for an interview at another company. Remember, the person that interviews you could expect you to perform the tasks stated on your resume but not qualified for or the contents in the resume may be verified. That's why you must make sure the details on your resume is fact not fiction.

THE SCREENING PROCESS

Typically there will be a preliminary telephone screening interview. The interviewer or HR personnel will call and ask you to come in for an interview. The purpose of the telephone interview is to see if you are the type of person that they want to ask in for a face-to-face interview. There are several things that will prepare you for that call. Here are a few tips for that call.

1. **Make sure you are in a quiet place when answering the telephone call.** If you are not in a quiet place where you can answer the telephone then let it go to voicemail. It is not professional to answer the telephone when on a crowded bus, a loud mall or a ball game. You may not be able to focus or schedule a call back. This will also be your first impression. It may be offensive that you didn't give them enough respect to speak with them in a professional setting. Don't Blow it! **REMEMBER: FIRST IMPRESSIONS ARE IMPORTANT!**

2. **Call back as soon as possible.** Listen to the message in its entirety and get all of the pertinent information from the message on a piece of paper and when you call back have that information handy. As soon as you are able to return the call, do so. Make sure that you are in quiet surroundings such as a

home office, bedroom or another room where there is total silence and you will be able to hear one another. Be professional. Know what position the caller was referring to when called. Here is an example of how to return the call.

"Hello, My name is Robert Spain and I am returning Janet Montgomery's call for the position of Director of Development. Is she available?"

When the person you are asking about gets to the telephone:

"Hello, Janet Montgomery, my name is Robert Spain and I am returning your call for the position of Director of Development."

When the HR person/Interviewer asks about the days and times that you are available, ask for their available days and times for interviewing. This will show that you are flexible. After a date and time is agreed upon, make sure you end on a good note such as:

"Mrs. Montgomery, is there anything special that I need to bring? Thank you for your time and I look forward to the interview on _____(date) at _____(time). Have a great day. Goodbye."

WHAT SHOULD I TAKE?

What to definitely take.

1. RESUMES AND REFERENCES:

You should take at least fifteen to twenty copies of your resume. The interviewer may not have a copy of your resume in front of him/her during the interview. By having an ample supply of resumes will show that you are organized and responsible. There may be two people to a full size panel of six or seven people who will interview you. It would be distracting for them if they had to share one resume. By having extra resumes, you can give each panel member an individual copy of your resume. Remember, just because the main interviewer may not hire you, one of the other interviewers may either be able to find a spot for you in their department or with another company that is looking for someone to fill a position. This interviewer may forward your information just based upon your resume. This is an advantage of allowing everyone to have their own copy of your resume. Also bring copies of your references along with your resume. This will allow them to check your character more quickly.

2. **DEGREES, CERTIFICATIONS AND LICENSES:**

    If you have obtained a college degree, certifications and/or licenses, make sure that you have a copy on hand. If you were in the military, definitely bring your DD 214. The interviewer may or may not ask to see any of these documents. However, it is better to have them and not need them, than to need them and not have them.

3. **PEN AND WRITING PAD:**

    Bring a pen and a writing pad. This serves several purposes. First, you can take notes throughout the interview so that you can ask specific questions at the end of the interview. Second, this also shows the interviewer that you are interested in the interview by taking notes. Lastly, this shows the interviewer your ability to be organized and prepared. This is a plus. *Ask if it is ok to take notes before doing so.*

4. **MINTS:**

    Bring mints to the interview because this will help keep your breath fresh. Small mints will be able to be hidden under your tongue if you are called after you put one in your mouth. Gum is a no-no.

What should I not bring?

1. **CHILDREN:**

    Although some employers may understand, it is professional suicide to bring children to an interview. The company that you are interviewing with does not want to have to worry about their receptionist entertaining a child for at least an hour. This will delay productivity of the company. Also, if the child gets injured, then the company is liable. This also gives the employer an indication of future problems that you may have with obtaining child care. If you cannot find child care, try and reschedule the interview.

2. THE COMPETITOR'S PRODUCTS:

Do not bring the competitor's products into the interview with you. This is considered disrespect and a slap in the face to the company in which you are interviewing. A pen and pad are good items to bring, but having a pen with the competitor's logo on it is interview suicide. You may like Burger King's shakes but do not bring it into McDonald's when going in for an interview.

3. CELL PHONES/IPODS:

In this technological world, many people feel as though that they are unable to live without their cell phone. Leave this technological device either in the car, in your briefcase or deep in your pocket. No matter where you leave it, make sure it is totally off, not on vibrate and completely out of sight. It is a sign of disrespect to the interviewer and the company if your cell phone goes off in the middle of the interview. If it is out of sight and off then you won't have the temptation to answer your phone or return a text. Nothing should disturb your opportunity to shine. It is also beneficial if you leave your iPod in the car or deep in your suitcase, portfolio or pocket if you don't have any other place to put it. This will prevent it from accidentally turning on. You do not want to be embarrassed by your IPod accidentally turning on with a song that is not appropriate.

4. GUM/CANDY:

I know you are saying that suggesting not bringing gum to an interview is a little outrageous. There is evidence that if you go to an interview with gum, you are more likely to forget to take it out of your mouth before you go into the interview room. Also, trying to hide the gum under your tongue could impair your speech, or even worse, it could fall out of your mouth. That would really make an impression on the interviewer, a negative one!

Candy is also discouraged from bringing to an interview. It do not freshen your breath. Plus, certain types of fruity flavored candy can have the reversed effect on your breath. As with gum, trying to hide candy under your tongue can lead to smacking which will leave the interviewer with a negative impression of you.

5. CIGARETTES:

If you are a smoker, then you should think about not smoking until after the interview. If you smoke before the interview then your clothes will have the smell of smoke. If you must smoke, then do it at home before leaving and brush your teeth afterwards to prevent the odor from clinging to your clothes, hair or breath. Remember, the interviewer may not be a smoker and the smell of smoke may offend that person.

6. COFFEE/SODAS:

If you must have coffee, consume it before you leave home and immediately brush your teeth. The reason for this, coffee leaves your breath in an undesirable manner. It also leaves a residue on your teeth. Brushing your teeth after drinking coffee will ensure that the interviewer will not be left with a bad impression with your coffee stained breath and teeth.

Sodas are no better to drink before an interview. Sodas have carbonation in them. This means that if you drink a soda right before the interview, then you will likely have a need to release the carbonation gases. The manner in which you release those carbonation gases can be disturbing and rude for you and the interviewer during the interview. To be on the safe side, if you are thirsty, drink water.

7. EXCESS BAGGAGE:

Interviewees who carry large loads of stuff to interviews may appear less professional and less organized than those who manage to leave the heavy equipment behind. If you do not exercise your best judgment, what you bring to the interview can cost you an offer. There will almost always be a designated storage area you can use. Consider closets, hotel suites, your car, empty classrooms, or receptionists' desks. Use them to store everything except your packet. This way, you will not waste valuable time trying to find a place for your things in the interviewing room. Women who want to carry their handbags to interviews should consider interviewing without them, unless they can find something that looks unobtrusive and professional. Brief cases or shoulder bags that is thin, dark, and medium-sized, without bright buckles or chains works best.

What is optional to bring?

1. WORK SAMPLES:

Make sure the work you bring is your best. Bring samples of your work if it is requested or relevant. Unless you are asked to bring original artwork, bring copies because you will be leaving them with the interviewer for further review later.

2. PANTYHOSE (WOMEN):

It is very embarrassing getting to the interview only to find out that you have a run in your pantyhose. If you bring an extra set, then you can be confident that if a run does occur, you won't have to worry about the interviewer seeing it. That will be one less thing to worry about and you can focus on the interview.

3. TRANSCRIPTS:

If you are just graduating from college or a vocational school, the employer may want to see your transcripts. Bring your transcripts just in case it is required. The reason for bringing your transcripts is that this is an indication of your work ethic and knowledge because you may not have a lot of experience. It is better to be prepared and not need it than to need it and not be prepared.

4. LAPTOP:

If your portfolio contains digital information, bring a laptop or some other medium with you. Do not expect your interviewer to supply necessary equipment unless agreed upon. Avoid carrying bulky objects as well. Do not overwhelm the interview room with all of your gear. Keep it simple and professional.

5. DEODORANT:

You can bring a travel size stick of deodorant just in case you are a sweater or your freshness has started to wear off. Make sure you freshen up before applying the deodorant. Make sure the deodorant does not have a strong scent because this can be very distracting to the interviewer. Remember, if you can smell it then the interviewer can too.

6. SMALL TUBE OF LOTION:

Bring a small tube of lotion with you. Depending on the season, especially in the winter the weather could dry your hands and face. Make sure it is hypo-allergenic and you apply it lightly. You do not know what the interviewer is allergic to. This will help the hand-shake go smoothly. An interviewer does not want to shake hands with someone whose hand is dry or oily. It doesn't look professional.

PERSONAL PRESENTATION

Hygiene is important!

The importance of good hygiene overall is something that needs to be discussed. Although, it should be a no brainer, during my research, hiring managers stressed that some candidates come into the interview with hygiene issues. Therefore, the issue of hygiene will be addressed in detail in this chapter. Good hygiene and clean/fresh inner and outer garments are a must.

1. **TAKE A SHOWER:**

   The night before the interview take a shower. Concentrate on the areas where odor tends to come from such as under your arms, private parts and your feet. The morning of the interview either take another shower or hit those crucial spots once again. Men pay special attention to the neckline. A ring around the collar during an interview is distracting and just plain unprofessional.

2. **BRUSH YOUR TEETH:**

   The night before the interview, brush your teeth and wash your mouth out with mouthwash. This will help kill some bacteria that appear throughout the night when you sleep. The morning of the interview, brush your teeth and wash your mouth out with mouth-wash once more. Take mints with you to the interview to keep your breath fresh. **DO NOT EAT ONIONS BEFORE YOUR INTERVIEW!** The smell of onions not only is hard to get off of your breath but the scent will get into your clothing also, especially if they are fresh onions.

3. TAKE CARE OF YOUR NAILS:

Many hiring managers notice the interviewee's finger nails. This tells a lot about a person. Make sure your nails are neatly clipped and clean. There should only be a clear color on your nails. Colorful nails are not recommended, also having long nails is perceived as unprofessional and immature.

4. MAKE SURE YOU SHAVE (MEN):

Shave on the night before the interview. This will be one less thing that you must do. This also allows the little nicks to heal and not bleed on your shirt. It is embarrassing if you walk into an interview and a piece of napkin is stuck to your face because you nicked your face while shaving and it hasn't stopped bleeding yet or a blood stain is on your shirt.

5. MAKE SURE YOUR CLOTHES ARE CLEAN:

Before you even think about going on an interview, make sure you have appropriate interview attire and everything fits correctly. The clothes that you are going to wear for the interview should be clean and free from odors, stains or dirt. Get your clothes ready the night before, so you don't have to spend time getting them ready on the day of the interview. If your clothes are "Dry Clean Only", take them to the cleaners after each interview, so they are ready for next time. Once your clothes are in order, make sure you do the same for your shoes. Polish your shoes.

If you do not have interview attire, then there are several places that you can go and purchase these items very inexpensively. Places like Sears and JC Penny are stores that have professional attire. The popular discount stores such as Wal-Mart, Kmart or Target are other stores to visit. If all fails, go to the local mom and pop clothing store or the Thrift Store. Your local Thrift Store is a good source of professional attire for pennies on the dollar.

What should I wear?

Appropriate dress is based on the company and the position you are applying for. Whenever in doubt, dress conservatively. The first impression you make on a potential employer is the most important one. You never get to make a second first impression. The first judgment an interviewer makes is going to be based on how you look and what you are wearing. That's why it's always important to dress professionally for a job interview, even if the work environment is casual. The best way to make sure you look professional is to stick with the "TRIPLE B RULE." The "TRIPLE B RULE" is to stick with the professional colors of "Blues (Navy), Browns and Blacks." Charcoal Grey is also an option. Women have a little more flexibility on the choice of colors. Remember to ask ahead of time what the expectation is on your attire. It is always preferable to over-dress for an interview unless you know the company has a strict casual environment. *Note: Most companies, no matter how qualified the applicant, will not hire males who's underwear is exposed.*

MEN INTERVIEW ATTIRE:

1. **Suit (solid color – navy blue, black, brown, or charcoal grey):**

   Make sure your suit is clean and has a proper fit. Navy Blue, Black, Brown, and Charcoal Grey are colors accepted and worn in the business world. Do not wear a Zoot Suit or a suit that is tailor made in a style that states, "I am going out for a night on the town," and instead of "I am going on an interview that will change my life." Your suit must look professional.

2. **Long sleeve shirt (white or coordinated with the suit):**

   Your shirt should be white or coordinated with your suit. Make sure the shirt compliments the suit and makes it looks professional. The shirt must be clean and pressed with no rings around the neck. This is why a man must pay special attention to the neckline when taking care of hygiene. You should not wear loud colors or of a shirt that has multiple colors. Remember, you are going to a job interview and not a nightclub.

3. **Belt:**

   If you are wearing a grey, black or navy suit, a black belt would be best. If you are wearing a brown suit, then a brown belt would be best to wear. This may seem trivial because you may never take off of your jacket. If you are in an environment where you must take off your jacket, then you want to match because this shows professionalism.

4. **Tie:**

   Just like the shirt, the tie must compliment the suit. It also must be professional. You can wear a tie with multiple colors in it, but make sure it matches the suit, does not have loud colors, and fits you correctly. If you have any doubts about if a tie that you have with multiple colors compliments the suit, then a solid color tie would be the best thing to wear.

5. **Dark socks, conservative leather shoes:**

The color and type of socks are very important. First of all, **DO NOT WEAR SWEAT SOCKS!** This will give the interviewer the impression that you are not taking the interview seriously enough to take the time to put on dark socks. This is very unprofessional. You must wear dark socks. They can be grey, navy, brown or black depending on the suit. If you have any doubts, then black socks are the safest thing to wear. Make sure that the socks are clean and odor free.

Shoes are very important. Make sure they are clean and polished. **DO NOT** wear cowboy boots, sandals, gym shoes, or suede shoes. The shoes that are worn must be leather and have a professional appearance. Make sure you air out your shoes and/or put some foot powder in them to remove any odor. Shoe odors can be very distracting. If you can smell the scent coming from your shoes, then everyone else can too. Shoe odors can be the reason that you do not receive an offer.

6. **Little or no jewelry:**

It is proper to wear a class ring, wedding band and a watch. If you must wear a chain with a religious emblem on it, put it on the inside where it is not seen. Although wearing multiple chains around your neck and multiple rings on both hands and 18 karat gold earrings in both ears is appropriate for the night club, but for the professional world, it is not.

7. **Neat, professional hairstyle:**

   Your hair is a part of your first impression. If your hair is not neatly trimmed, then that could be a strike against you. This will give the impression to the interviewer that you didn't believe that the interview was important enough to take the time to get a nicely trimmed professional haircut. If you have a lot of hair, it is not necessary to have all of it cut off. Make sure that it is neatly trimmed and DO NOT wear braids or corn rolls to the interview. This is a sign of immaturity and unprofessionalism. If you have dread locks, make sure that they are clean and neat.

8. **Limit the aftershave and/or cologne:**

   Although the ladies in the club or your wife might love your new cologne, it is best not to wear any to the interview. Good old fashion smell of soap and water will be sufficient. You will have less of a chance of not putting on too much and overwhelming the interviewer if you do not wear any at all. But, if you insist on wearing aftershave or cologne, then put on a very minimal amount. A person should not be able to smell the scent unless they are within 2 to 4 inches of your personal space.

9. **Neatly trimmed nails:**

   As stated before, it is of the utmost importance that your nails are clean and neatly trimmed. Your nails tell a lot about your hygiene habits.

10. **Tattoos:**

    Cover all visible tattoos if possible. If they are on your hands or your face, be prepared to explain the reason why they are in those visible places. Do not be surprised if having visible tattoos are the reason for not receiving the offer. If tattoos are political, radical, sexual in nature, large or have multiple tattoos, make sure you cover them no matter where they are.

11. Portfolio or briefcase:

Make sure you have a light briefcase or portfolio case. This will hold all of your pertinent documents and keep you organized. Professionalism is important and having a light briefcase or portfolio will enhance your professional appearance. Remember, having a positive first impression is crucial. This will help you with the first impression.

WOMEN'S INTERVIEW ATTIRE:

1. Suit (navy, black, brown or charcoal grey):

Make sure your suit is clean and has a proper fit. Form fitting (tight) or very loose fitting suits may not make the best first impression. Navy, black, brown, and charcoal grey are colors accepted and worn in the business world. The suit skirt should be long enough and loose enough so you can sit comfortably during the interview.

2. Coordinated blouse:

Women have more flexibility on what color blouse they can wear. Although this may be true, your blouse should complement the suit. Loud colors are a professional no-no. The style of the blouse should also be conservative. Cleavage may be appropriate for the night club, but it is not for an interview. Remember, you want the interviewer to look at your eyes and not at your cleavage. Wearing an appropriate blouse will help you avoid awkward situations.

3. Conservative shoes:

Clean closed-toe shoes are the very best option you can have. Although hills are acceptable, make sure they are no more than 2". If you do not have experience with walking in heels, the day of your interview is not the time to gain experience. Make sure the shoes are polished and clean. **DO NOT** wear sandals, gym shoes, cowboy boots, or open-toed shoes.

4. No or Limited jewelry:

As with the blouse, women have more flexibility with jewelry. The appropriate pieces, if you must wear jewelry, are small studded earrings, a watch, wedding rings and a class ring. No dangling earrings or arms full of bracelets. If you must wear a chain with a religious emblem on it, then put it on the inside of your blouse out of sight. If you can't put it inside your blouse where it can't be seen, then avoid wearing it into the interview. No jewelry is better than inappropriate or too much jewelry.

5. Professional hairstyle:

Your hair is part of your first impression. Having a neat professional hairstyle is important. When accepting the invitation for an interview, carefully examine your hairstyle and ask yourself, "Would I hire myself with a hairstyle like this?" If the answer is no, then you must reconsider the type of hairstyle that you have. Also, abnormal and loud colors such as red, blue, orange, green, purple, etc., is inappropriate when interviewing. You want the interviewer to focus on your qualifications, not your hair. Overwhelming hair color/styles should be avoided.

6. Neutral pantyhose:

Neutral pantyhose are the best way to go in an interview. Other color pantyhose may be too trendy. Neutral pantyhose complement all professional attire. Remember to bring an extra pair just in case you have a run in the pair that you are wearing.

7. Light make-up and perfume:

Make-up is to enhance the natural beauty of women. When interviewing, it is best to apply your make-up lightly. There are several reasons for this. First, if you apply a heavy amount of make-up, then there is a greater chance for it to ruin your clothes. Yet, most importantly, if you wear heavy amounts of make-up, then it may be a distraction to the interviewer.

Although you and your family might love the scent of your new perfume, wearing it to the interview is discouraged. The smell of regular soap and water is sufficient. This will keep you from putting on too much and overwhelming the interviewer. If you must wear perfume, the scent should only be noticeable within 2 to 4 inches of your personal space.

8. Neatly manicured clean nails:

When you accept the invitation for an interview, look at your nails to see if they are appropriate for an interview. If not, then seriously consider changing them. Your nails should be clean, neatly trimmed and a reasonable length. The color should be clear. Wearing nail colors to match your suit or blouse is considered too trendy and therefore, inappropriate for an interview. The wearing of studs and nail rings are strongly discouraged also.

9. Portfolio or briefcase:

Make sure you have a light briefcase or portfolio case. This will hold all of your pertinent documents and keep you organized. Professionalism is important and having a light briefcase or portfolio will enhance your professional appearance. Remember, having a positive first impression is crucial. This will help with your first impression.

LOCATION AWARENESS

Time Management

One of the most important things that you must understand is that time management is crucial. This is a sign of being organized. Take care of hygiene the night before and on the day of the interview. Lay out your clothes the night before and make sure that they are appropriate interview attire. Having all of the required documents such as your resume, certifications, licenses, degrees, pen and pad are in your portfolio or light briefcase. You must know the pertinent information about the company that you are interviewing with and know what is on your resume. Having these things done prior to the day of the interview will save you a lot of time and stress. This will help you focus on the interview. Now that all of those things are taken care of, you are not done yet.

Location of the interview

Know the exact address of where you are going for the interview. The interview location is not always the place where you sent your resume. When talking to the person that offered you the interview confirm the location of the interview and make sure you write the address down. It is wise to contact the person that is interviewing you or the person that offered the interview to confirm the location of the interview if not already known. This does not make you look stupid. This will show the interviewer that you are not afraid of seeking help when unsure of something. This may just work in your favor.

Know how long it takes to get there

Now that you have the address, you must figure out how to get to and how long it will take to arrive at the interview site. There are several resources that you can use. The internet is the best way to figure this out. The use of websites such as MapQuest or your local public transit websites can be beneficial because it gives you at least three routes and the approximate times. Print out the directions. If you do not have access to the internet, then acquire a city map or bus and train schedules.

The next step is to take a trip to the interview site. This should be done before the day of the interview and around the time you will be leaving for the interview. This will help you determine what time would be the best time to leave on the day of the interview. *Rule of thumb: leave the actual time + thirty minutes.* For instance, if it takes you an actual hour to get to the interview site, add thirty minutes and leave one and one half hours before you are due for the interview. This will help you plan for unexpected incidents, such as, forgetting your portfolio or being caught in traffic because of an accident or train. This will give you enough time to either take an alternate route, (*this is the reason for printing different routes*) or just weather the traffic until you are able to move smoother and quicker without being pressed for time. This will also give you a chance to freshen up and gain your composure before you enter the interview. Remember you want to put your best foot forward and create a fantastic first impression.

THE ARRIVAL

Check your hygiene

It is the day of the interview. Make sure that you get enough sleep the night before. Now that you have arrived at the interview site, go directly to the restroom and freshen yourself up. Check your hygiene, from your breath to your feet. Now is the time to closely look yourself over to find imperfections from major to minor. Your clothes should still be neat and professional.

Be professional at all times

It is important to maintain your professionalism at all times. Once you enter the interview site make sure you have a pleasant demeanor, smile and speak clearly and professionally. If you are on the elevator with someone, always assume that the person riding with you is the interviewer. It is very embarrassing to have a negative conversation on the elevator and the interviewer is the person that was on the elevator. (*Remember, you never get a second chance to make a first impression*). It is also important to be nice and professional to the gatekeeper. Whether you know it or not, the gatekeeper is a very important person in that office. He/she may determine your fate before you enter the interview room. The gatekeeper is referred to as the receptionist or secretary of the interviewer. Often the interviewer will ask the opinion of the receptionist or secretary on your professionalism before he/she meets you formally.

Do not speak negatively (bad mouth) about former employers or talk unnecessarily

There will probably be other candidates present interviewing for the same position. It is encouraged to have small talk with the other candidates. While engaging in conversation with the other candidates, do not bad mouth former employers regardless if the opportunity presents itself. Let everyone else participate in negative talk. Remember, the gatekeeper is listening to every word you are saying. It may appear as though they are not paying any attention to the conversation but they are.

REMEMBER...

Once you arrive, check your hygiene and freshen up. Have a pleasant demeanor and smile. Do not engage in negative conversations because it may come back to haunt you. Overall be professional at all times.

THE ACTUAL INTERVIEW

Come in and have a seat

Participating in mock interviews before the actual interview date is helpful. A mock interview is designed to help you relax and know what to expect in an actual interview. It helps you prepare so that when you enter into the interview room, there is some familiarity in the interviewing process. If you are unable to participate in a mock interview, then look in the mirror and ask yourself questions, ask a friend or family member to ask you questions so that you can get a feel of the interview.

When you enter the interview room, you will be judged on three basic things. These things are your appearance, non-verbal communication and verbal communication skills. All three things speak volumes about who you are. We cannot stress enough about your appearance. You are on stage at this point. It's time to wow the interviewer and get the offer.

NON-VERBAL COMMUNICATIONS

People have learned to interpret body language throughout their lives. Non-verbal communication is powerful. A frown can be interpreted as the person is angry or is having a bad day. A smile and a spring in the step of a person can be interpreted as happy or having a wonderful day. Sometimes body language sends the wrong non-verbal signal. This is why it is important to send the correct non-verbal signals.

Use positive body language to your advantage

Handshake

Give a firm handshake. A limp handshake will be interpreted as not having confidence in oneself. On the opposite side, a bone crushing handshake will be interpreted as being too confident and as a challenge of strength. A firm handshake should be given to a woman as well as a man. The dainty handshake to a woman will not impress her. This type of handshake could insult her. This will be interpreted as her being inferior to a man. This is not the signal that you want to send to a potential female employer. A handshake will either increase or decrease your credibility.

The proper way to execute a handshake is to extend your hand with confidence. The meaty part of your hand is inserted to the meaty part of the other person's hand. Firmly close your hand, shake and then release. Do not squeeze to crush the other person's hand. While shaking the interviewer's hand, accompany it with eye contact and a pleasant smile.

Do Not Sit Until Invited

Do not sit until the interviewer invites you to sit. If you sit before invited will show a sign of disrespect. It is the same as someone coming into your home, walking in and sitting down before being invited by you. This is a sign of total disrespect and can destroy your chances of getting an offer.

Make eye contact

Making good eye contact is crucial to achieving effective non-verbal communication. It conveys that you really care about what the interviewer is saying. It also displays that you are confident, intelligent, competent and honest. Do not stare at the interviewer. Look at him/her while they are talking. Avoid moving your eyes from side to side and looking down. This will give the indication that you are unsure of yourself and/or possibly hiding something. Look at the interviewer's forehead if you are uncomfortable looking him/her directly in his/her eyes. This will give the illusion that you are looking them in the eyes. If there is a panel of interviewers, periodically make eye contact with each one.

Have good posture

Having good posture is vital. When entering the interview room, walk tall, stand tall and most importantly sit tall. A person's posture is a sign of confidence and power potential. When sitting, sit on the edge of your chair and lean slightly forward. When standing up, stand straight up. This will speak volumes about your interest, motivation and confidence.

Facial Expressions

Facial expressions are important. Many are unaware of the facial expressions that they have. Having a pleasant demeanor will help you diminish the unpleasant expressions you may have because of your anxiety of the interview. The interviewer understands that you will be nervous but he does not want to see it on your face. **SMILE** ☺ and appear to be confident. You do not have to have a continuous smile on your face but continue to bring it back and make sure it is genuine.

Gestures

Do not use gestures to stress the importance of your points. When you do use gestures, make sure it comes off as natural and meaningful instead of theatrical. **DO NOT FIDGET.** If you are nervous and unable to control your gestures, **clasp your hands together and place them in your lap.**

Personal Space

Make sure you recognize and identify the boundaries of your personal space and others also. Their personal space may be smaller than yours. If this is the case, do not pull back or move away. Hang in there, breathe, bear it and relax.

Demonstrate confidence, pride and enthusiasm

Act as though you want and deserve the job. Be careful as to not appear desperate or cocky. The candidate's level of enthusiasm often influences the interviewer's decision on whether or not to hire the candidate.

Taking Notes

Ask if it is ok to take notes before doing so. Make sure you take notes. This will do several things. First of all, it will let the interviewer know that you are genuinely interested in what they are saying. Secondly, it will give you an opportunity to formulate more questions. Lastly, it will help you tailor your answers around the information that was given.

VERBAL COMMUNICATION

Use verbal communication to your advantage

Through verbal communication, our goal is to have people understand what we are saying. Unlike written words, where people can go back and reread something several times, only 10% of spoken words get through to others (Menechella). Start your communication off right. Speak clearly and with confidence. Use the interviewer's name in your greeting. This displays respect for the interviewer. This will increase your likability and credibility instantly.

State your name and the position for which you are interviewing

The interviewer may interview for different positions. When you enter the interviewer's office, start with a friendly greeting by stating your name and the position you are interviewing for: *"Hello, Mr. Johnson, I'm Jerry Cole. I'm here to interview for the marketing position."* If you are already introduced by someone else just say: *"Hello, Mr. Johnson. I am here to interview for the marketing position."*

Project a clear and pleasant tone of voice

Make sure you use a friendly, courteous and pleasant tone of voice. This will create a positive reflection of your attitude. This will keep you from offending the interviewer. Remember, sometimes it is not what you say but how you say it.

Use Standard English

Correct grammar is essential to the success of the interview. Avoid slang, grammatical errors and common phrases (such as *you know*). Using incorrect grammar conveys immaturity and insecurity. It also may annoy the interviewer. Use correct grammar, word choice and businesslike vocabulary. Before the interview, have someone help you identify any grammatical weakness that you may possess.

Use positive words and phrases

Keep the content positive. Avoid words and phrases that take away your credibility such as *Just, only, I guess* and *probably.*

- ***Just*** and ***only*** minimizes the work that you have done. It also states that you are not proud of your work and implies that it wasn't meaningful. Any work that you have done is meaningful. It shows initiative.
- ***I guess*** implies uncertainty.
- ***Probably*** implies doubt in your abilities.

Keep the interview businesslike

The purpose for the interview is to see if you and the company are a good fit for each other. Personal problems such as financial and domestic are inappropriate. Keep your focus professional.

Relax

One of the most important things to do is just **RELAX**. It is understandable to be nervous. If you are tense, then your body will show it.

Get a good night's sleep, If possible, allow extra time to exercise the day of the interview because this will relax your muscles and give you more energy during the day. During the interview, occasionally change positions but do not make any sudden movements. Do not forget to **SMILE** ☺. This is an effective way to break the tension for you and the interviewer.

NOW IT'S TIME TO TALK

STANDARD QUESTIONS

Now that you are inside the interview room in front of the interviewer, the questions are about to begin. There are some standard questions that almost all interviewers ask. You are at the edge of the chair, very attentive and ready for anything. It is time to shine. The very first question the interviewer asks is: ***"Tell me a little bit about yourself."*** You should have a 30 -60 second commercial already prepared. This is the time to tell about your outstanding accomplishments and not about your family history or personal life. Here is an example of what not to say.

> *"My name is Sally Johnson. I am a single mother of 5. I have three boys and two girls. My two oldest are in high school. My next two are in elementary school and I have a 4 year old. I am a very organized person. I juggle cleaning the house, cooking and helping the children with their homework because my ex-husband left two years ago. I have been out of work for about a year now. Before I was laid off, I worked for Manly Advertising Company for 6 years as an account manager. So I have managerial experience."*

Although this is a story that could be heartfelt by the interviewer, this is not the purpose of this question. The purpose of this question is to see if you could convey your experiences (that are relevant to the job) to the interviewer effectively. Here is an effective answer to this question.

"I have a Bachelors of Science Degree in Marketing from Chicago State University with a 3.7 grade point average. After school, I worked two internships. The first one was with EZ Accounting as a Business Development Intern. My duties were to develop collateral material and marketing strategies. As a result of my efforts, there was a 30% increase in customer traffic. That internship lasted 2 years. My second internship was with Rocky Road Advertising Company. I was the webmaster intern and was responsible for the development of new strategies to drive new customers to their website. As a result of my internship, they had an increase of 8% of customers to their website. That internship lasted 1 year. As a result of the internship, I was offered employment with Manly Advertising Company. There I performed in various positions such as account manager for several accounts, project manager, senior account manager and senior project manager. As a result of my employment, the company grossed over $20 million over the 6 years I was there."

After that icebreaking question, a series of standard questions will follow. Some questions about your skills, education and work experiences will be asked such as:

- **What are your strongest skills?**

  Ideal Answer: Think over your accomplishments and your 30-60 second commercial and relate your skills to the position that you are applying.

- **Why do you want this job?**

  Ideal Answer: "My skills and experience are directly related to this position. I also have a passion for this field." Then give examples of your past job performances, experiences and education that are directly related to the position. This should be an indication of what you can do to for the company.

- **Why should I hire you? / Why do you think that you are the best candidate for this Job?**

  Ideal Answer: Your answer should be short and to the point. It should highlight the areas from your background that relate to current needs and problems. Recap the interviewer's description of the job, meeting it point by point with your skills. Make sure your answer focuses on how you can benefit the company with your qualifications.

- **What did you like/dislike about your last job?**

  Ideal Answer: The interviewer is looking for incompatibilities. Most interviews start with a preamble by the interviewer about the company. Pay attention! That information will help you answer this question. In fact, any statement the interviewers make about the job or corporation can be used to your advantage. So, in answer, you liked everything about your last job. You might even say your company taught you the importance of certain keys from the business, achievement, or professional profile. Criticizing a prior employer is a warning flag that you could be a problem employee. No one intentionally hires trouble, and that's what's behind the question. Keep your answer short and positive. For example, the only thing your past employer could not offer might be something like *"the ability to contribute more in different areas*"You might continue with, *"I really liked everything about the job. The reason I want to leave it is to find a position where I can make a greater contribution. You see, I worked for a large company that encourages specialization of skills. The smaller environment you have here will, allow me to contribute far more in different areas."* Tell them what they want to hear.

- **What is your greatest weakness?**

  Ideal Answer: Never say that you do not have a weakness. This may indicate to the interviewer that you are arrogant enough to think that you do not have weaknesses. Everyone has a weakness. This may be a skill that you lack. Tell the interviewer what weakness you have and how you are stregnthening that weakness. (i.e. through practice, planning, education and so on.)

- **Have you ever been fired or asked to resign from a job?**

  Ideal Answer: If you have been fired, use the term laid off. This sounds less negative. Be honest about the reason for termination. Briefly explain the situation and circumstances and end on a positive note. Tell what you learned from the situation.

  If you were laid off for a legitimate reason such as downsizing, a loss of company business or a lagging economy, then this question does not apply to you. Also if you quit, this question does not apply to you.

BEHAVIORAL QUESTIONS

In a behavioral interview, an employer knows what skills are needed in the candidate they wish to hire and will ask questions to find out if the candidate possesses those skills. Instead of asking how you would behave in a particular situation, the interviewer will ask how you did behave. The interviewer will want to know how you handled a situation, instead of what you might do in the future.

Preparing for a behavioral interview.

It may sometimes be difficult to prepare for a behavioral interview because the uncertainty of what questions are going to be asked. The best way to prepare for this type of interview is to think about all of your previous work experiences that are related to the job description. Prepare stories that illustrate times when you have successfully solved problems or performed memorably. These stories will be helpful with your responses that are meaningfully in a behavioral interview. If the interviewer asks you a question that you do not understand, then ask for clarification. It is better to ask for clarification than to give an unrelated or inappropriate answer to the question asked.

When you do answer a question, make sure you follow this format:

- Identify a specific situation
- Give the tasks that needed to be done
- The action you took

- The results (i.e. what happened)

- What you learned from the results (if applicable)

THE TOP 10 BEHAVIORAL INTERVIEW QUESTIONS

According to the interview guide Allison Doyle of About.com, here are the top 10 behavioral interview questions.

- Have you handled a difficult situation? How?

- Give an example of a goal you reached and tell me how you achieved it.

- Tell me about how you worked effectively under pressure.

- Share an example of how you were able to motivate employees or co-workers.

- Describe a decision you made that wasn't popular and how you handled implementing it.

- How do you handle a challenge? Give an example.

- Have you ever made a mistake? How did you handle it?

- Give an example of how you set goals and achieve them.

- Give an example of how you worked on a team.

- What do you do if you disagree with someone at work?

There will be follow-up questions also. You may be asked what you did, what you said, how you reacted, or how you felt. The rules for the initial questions still apply. Listen carefully to the questions being asked. Be honest, detailed and clear with your answers. Remember, there are no wrong or right answers. The interviewer is only trying to see if your skills fit the position that he/she is trying to fill.

During an interview, you may find that the questions may be challenging. Here are some tips for answering these questions.

- Identify anything that would be of a concern to the interviewer on your resume.

- Plan your responses carefully.

- The way you respond is just as important as the response itself.

- Stay calm and unflustered. Answer the questions in a calm and professional manner.

- Beware of your tone of voice. Do not be defensive or aggressive.

- Use body language that conveys that you are comfortable and confident.

- Be concise and do not ramble on because this displays nervousness.

- Be brief but make sure you have addressed any concerns the interviewer has. It is important that the interviewer feels comfortable that the question has been dealt with properly so that the interview can move on.

RESPONDING TO
DIFFICULT QUESTIONS

During an interview, you may be faced with the challenge of answering questions about salary requirements, gaps in your employment and why you were laid off or fired. The answers to these questions are very important and can have a huge impact on the interview. Therefore, here are some tips from www.best-job-interview.com, on answering these questions:

THE SALARY QUESTION

It is often awkward when an interviewer asks that question about the salary you expect to receive. It may be easier for the candidate who has a salary history in a particular industry, but for the candidate that does not have a salary history in the particular industry, due to reasons such as a recent graduate or a change of career field, this question if unprepared, could be very difficult.

For the candidate that does not have a salary history in that industry or a salary history at all, here are some guidelines when asked about salary requirements.

- Research the salary in that industry in relation to that position.

- Give a salary range to the employer.

- Make sure the range can be backed up with details on how you got your figure.

There are some research tools that you can use in order to know what type of salary is paid to candidates that are just starting in the industry. www.salary.com, www.salaryexpert.com and The National Association of Colleges and Employers website, www.naceweb.org, www.payscale. com and www.vault.com are some tools that can be used to research industry relevant salaries.

For the candidate that does have a salary history, according to best-job-interview.com, if this question is asked early in the interview process, indicate that you are interested in learning more about the position and there is time later for discussing salary. If the interviewer is persistent, then try the following techniques:

- Ask if there is a salary grade for that position

- Ask if there have been an amount budgeted for the position

If there is not a specific amount and the interviewer is pressing for a number, then you can do the following:

- *"The range for this sort of position is $X and $Y."*

- *"I am currently earning $X..., I would love to better that figure but my main interest is the actual position."*

Remember, that you do not want to not give an amount if the interviewer presses you for an answer because you may create the impression that you do not care what pay that is received and any offer is acceptable. Also, you do not want to undervalue yourself. Here are the factors to consider what range is appropriate:

- The salary that you want

- Your current salary

- The market-related salary for that position

When stating your salary history, if asked, be truthful. The interviewer may verify that salary with your previous employer. Make sure that it is not perceived that money is your primary motivation. Always emphasize your interest in the position itself.

THE GAP IN YOUR EMPLOYMENT HISTORY QUESTION

There are instances where a person may have gaps in their employment history. Those instances may be caring for an ill parent or child, pregnancy, raising children, or a job search that has taken longer than anticipated. Regardless of the reason, the fact still remains that there have been gaps in your employment history and the interviewer will question the time outside the workforce.

Short periods of unemployment such as for study or job transition is often self-explanatory and is understood by the interviewer. Also, a longer period for about a year with a solid work history prior to that will often be (but not guaranteed) overlooked. The longer period of time and how often those gaps occur will bring concerns to a potential employer of your reliability and commitment level. Therefore, this will need some clarification. Here are some simple and easy suggestions on how to answer the "gap in employment history" question.

<u>First of all, be honest.</u> Making up reasons why there have been gaps in your employment history could come back to haunt you. Employers will most often check your work history and verify any information that you give them. So be honest.

During this period, if you have taken a class, volunteered, consulted or even some contract work, this will be looked upon as being favorable. This shows that during this period, you have been not only searching for employment but you were improving yourself and kept active.

The answer ***"for personal reasons"*** often raises a red flag to the interviewer. This answer is open to a wide range of misinterpretations. This may be misinterpreted that you are a problem employee and are not able to work well with others. Clarification will often be required. Avoid sounding defensive. Acknowledge the interviewer's concern.

"I fully understand that you need to know what I was doing during that time, and I would like to discuss this with you."

Appear composed and unapologetic, this will reassure the interviewer that you are comfortable with your reasons and that they should be too.

If you have been looking for employment for an extended period of time, explain to the interviewer that you have been looking for a company for long term employment and not just a pay check. Then, explain how this company and the position that you are interviewing for is the right one for you and the company as well.

Finally, focus on the positive things that you have done during this period. If you have taken a class, taught classes, volunteered, consulted or traveled, inform the interviewer. This shows your initiative and that you weren't just sitting around while searching for your next job.

THE LAID OFF, FIRED AND TERMINATION QUESTION

This is often the most difficult question to answer in an interview. The terms laid off, fired and termination have a negative sound to it. Laid off is less damaging as terminated and fired.

There is a difference between being laid off and being fired or terminated. Being laid off is something that was beyond your control. For example, the company may have eliminated your position or your whole department due to downsizing. Another aspect of being laid off could be the company may have gone out of business. Here are some tips to answering the question about being laid off.

- Keep these answers as short as possible.
- Do not be bitter or angry. This will only show that you are a complainer.
- Keep a positive attitude about the layoff.
- Briefly discuss what you have been doing (i.e. took a class, volunteered, consulted etc.)
- Highlight what you accomplished while you were there.
- Explain that you are eager to face new challenges.

Termination (being fired) from a job is due to some type of disciplinary actions against you-the employee. If this is the case for your unemployment, it may be more difficult to explain. Here are some tips to get through this tough question.

- Be honest. Do not mislead the interviewer by telling them you were terminated for something different. Employment verification will tell the correct reason for termination.

- Be aware of your body language and your tone of voice.

- Keep positive. Do not talk negative about your ex-co-workers or ex- boss.

- If there was a problem with a co-worker or boss, say *"we"* showing accountability for your actions also. This shows maturity.

- Trying to defend yourself will only result in an awkward and prolong discussion on a negative issue.

- Be brief and concentrate on the things that you can do for the company that matches your skill set.

Prepare answers that you are comfortable with and practice them. Make sure you are comfortable with the wording and or phrasing of your answers. If you are not, then reword or rephrase your answer until you are comfortable with it. The termination from a job does not eliminate you automatically from getting hired by another company. The important thing is your attitude toward the situation. If you have a positive attitude toward the situation, show that you have learned from the experience and have become wiser from it will help you get through this tough question.

QUESTIONS THE INTERVIEWER SHOULD BE ASKED

When the interviewer is satisfied with all of your answers or is done asking you questions, they will ask you if you have any questions for them. Rule of thumb: **ALWAYS ASK QUESTIONS!** This is also another chance for your research to pay off which will help you write down appropriate questions to ask the interviewer. Prepare at least three to five questions. Make sure the questions are thoughtful and are not easily found in places such as the company's website. Keep the questions positive. Do not wait until the end to ask all of your questions. If possible, casually interject some questions that are appropriate to that stage of the interview. Remember, you are not just being interviewed. You are interviewing the company to see if you are a right fit for each other.

Here are some examples of some questions that you can ask:

- Do you have a training program for this position? If so, please describe it for me.

- Will the responsibilities of this position expand with time and experience on the job?

- How would you describe a typical work day/week in this position?

- What are the prospects of growth in this company?

- What do you like about working here?

- What are you looking for in a candidate?

- What is the next step in the interview process?

- When can I expect to hear from you?

Just like there are questions that can be asked, there are questions that are a no-no. Asking the wrong questions can be the determining factor if you get a second interview or an offer of employment.

Here are some examples of questions that are simply a no-no:

- What does the company do?

- Will I have an office?

- How much sick time and vacation time will I get?

- When will I be eligible for a raise?

- Can I change my schedule if I get the job?

- Did I get the job?

HAVE A NICE DAY.
THE FOLLOW-UP

Now that you have been through the toughest part of the interview, you think that you can take a deep breath. Not just yet. Your very last question should be, *"When can I expect to hear from you?"* When the interviewer gets up to walk you out, graciously stand straight up, extend your hand and give a firm hand shake, make eye contact and have a pleasant look on your face. Do not forget to thank the interviewer for taking the time out of their busy schedule to interview you. Although, you may want to run or walk very quickly out of the office, DO NOT! Walk at an even and professional pace because you do not want to send the message of wanting to get away from the interviewer. This will send the wrong message. Remember, your interview is not over. You are being observed in everything you do while in the company's facility.

For example: If you have interviewed for a position in the transportation industry, do not go into the parking lot and peel off to celebrate a great interview. Although, there was an indication that you may get the job, a stunt like this could lose the job for you. This type of behavior displays immaturity.

It is time for the follow-up.

An interview follow-up can increase your chances of getting the job by 30%. An interviewer interprets a follow-up as the candidate taking the initiative and show interest in the job. (Levitt) Many candidates do not bother to take the initiative to follow-up. This is a fatal error. This will make you stand out from the other candidates.

There are several ways to follow-up after an interview. These are by telephone, email, written letter or in person. A rule of thumb is to follow-up within 24 hours of the interview. This will keep your name on the interviewer's mind.

In your follow-up letter or email, thank the interviewer for the opportunity for the interview. Make sure you reinforce your qualifications and anything that you want to either clear up or any questions that you may have forgotten. Remember, keep it brief. Before you pop up in person or by telephone, get the interviewer's ok to follow up by these methods. The person may be busy and do not have time to talk on the telephone or speak with you in person. If you follow-up by telephone, send a thank you note also without reinstating your qualifications.

If more than one person interviewed you, then send a different thank you letter to each one of them. Make sure the contents vary just in case they compare notes.

If the interviewer do not contact you by the specified date that was given about the decision of the position would be made, follow-up by telephone.

CONCLUSION

The acquisition of employment is somewhat difficult in this recovering economy due to the overwhelming number of qualified candidates. Employers are searching for the right candidate by various means. Understanding what employers want in an interview will give you a competitive advantage over other candidates. The information in this guide provided you with the tools to help navigate through the interviewing process with ease. NOW GO GET THAT JOB!!

SOCIAL NETWORKING
(Appendix A)

Social Networking is one of the most popular pass times today. The idea of connecting with old colleagues, military or college buddies is intriguing. This technological advancement can be a blessing; also it can be a curse. According to Erin Joyce of Investopedia.com, approximately 30% of employers use Facebook to screen potential employees. There are over 400 million active members on Facebook, making this the most popular social networking site to date. Social Networks such as Facebook, Twitter and LinkedIn can be an asset to have for employment purposes. Using these networking websites the correct way is crucial. Here are some social networking no-no's.

Do Not Have Inappropriate Pictures

Although chugging beer through a beer bong or posing in a sexy outfit provocatively maybe fun, potential employers will not see it this way. If hired, you are representing the company that you work for at all times, so therefore that type of negative behavior can be seen as immature and irresponsible. This can possibly have a negative effect on business.

Do Not Post Statuses That You Wouldn't Want Your Boss To See

You should avoid statuses such as *"Bill is going to call off to go to the football game tomorrow."* or *"After work I am going to the bar and get totally plastered tonight."* Anything that shows you as being deceitful, unreliable and unprofessional, could hurt your potential of getting that new job you applied for.

Do Not Complain About Your Current Job

Everyone has complained about their job at least once or twice but doing it in a public forum is not the best thing to do. Writing how a co-worker always show up late, how incompetent your boss is or how you hate your job may be innocent to you. Just like in the interview, trash talking about your job or co-workers is a big no-no. This could potentially put you in a position where you may lose your job and it sends a bad impression to a potential employer.

Do Not Post Conflicting Information Than On Your Resume

If you have in your resume that you have a bachelor's degree and on your profile, you have an associate's degree; you will most likely be immediately taken off of the interview list. You will be looked upon from careless to a liar. You do not want your integrity in question.

Not Understanding Your Security Settings

Many people do not fully understand these settings, or don't bother to check who has access to what. If you are going to use a social networking site (Facebook, Twitter or even LinkedIn) professionally, and even if you aren't, make sure you take the time to go through your privacy options. It is now possible to customize lists of friends and decide what each list can and cannot see. At the very least, your profile should be set so that people who are not your friend cannot see any of your pictures or information.

Losing By Association

You can't control what your friends post to your profile (although you can remove it once you see it), nor what they post to their own profiles or to those of mutual friends. If a potential employer sees those Saturday night pictures your friend has tagged you in where he is falling down drunk, it reflects poorly on you, even if the picture of you is completely innocent. It's unfortunate, but we often judge others by the company they keep, at least to some extent. Take a look at everything connected to your profile, and keep an eye out for anything you wouldn't want to show your mother.

Social Networking sites are like a two edged sword. On one side, if used very effectively, they can get you a job. On the other side, if used carelessly, they can either get you fired or not afford you the opportunity for that interview. Employers often use social networking sites to help determine the eligibility of a candidate. Is it right for them to do? Maybe or maybe not, but the fact still remains, this is a tool that is used. The best advice is to set your personal profile so that only friends you approve can see anything on that profile. Then, create a second, public profile on the same social network site purely for professional use. This profile functions like an online resume, and should only contain information you'd be comfortable telling your potential employer face to face. Having a social networking profile is a good thing – it presents you as technologically and professionally savvy. Just make sure your profile is helping to present your best side – not the side that got drunk at your girlfriend's birthday party.

INTERVIEWING CHECKLIST
(Appendix B)

RESEARCH COMPANY   ☐
History
Awards
Charitable Affiliations

UPDATE YOUR RESUME   ☐
Any new experience or education
Proofread

GATHER ESSENTIAL DOCUMENTS   ☐
Resumes
Letters of Recommendations
Transcripts
Certificates
Original or copied work (if applicable)

DRESS FOR SUCCESS   ☐
Take care of hygiene
Appropriate Business clothing
Appropriate fitting clothing
Clean clothing

KNOW THE LOCATION AND HOW TO GET THERE ☐

Get the correct interview address

Get directions (primary and alternate routes)

Know how long it takes to get to interview site form each route

Allow enough time for unforeseen events

THE ARRIVAL ☐

BE ON TIME!!!

Freshen up

Be professional

Review company's history, awards and charitable affiliations ☐

Review your pre-written questions ☐

THE ACTUAL INTERVIEW ☐

Be attentive

Take notes

Be enthusiastic!!!!

TIME TO TALK ☐

Think before you answer

Be clear and concise

Be honest

Be enthusiastic!!!!

YOUR TURN TO ASK QUESTIONS ☐

Have questions prepared

Ask Questions!!!!

Do not ask questions that have already been answered before this point in the interview.

THE FOLLOW UP ☐

Send an email within 24 hours thanking the interviewer for their time and inform them of anything that you may have missed during the interview.

Send a hand written note within 48 hours of interview thanking the interviewer for their time.

LIST OF QUESTIONS
(Appendix C)

There are plenty of interview questions that you might be asked depending upon the interviewer and/or job. Will you be asked every question? Probably not. Knowing the possible and probable questions that will be asked will help tremendously. Here is a listing of interview questions that will help you prepare. I know that this list may seem a little overwhelming, but the more familiar you are with these questions, the better your chances of acing the interview.

A List of Interview Questions

Basic Interview Questions:

- Tell me about yourself.
- What are your strengths?
- What are your weaknesses?
- Why do you want this job?
- Where would you like to be in your career five years from now?
- What's your ideal company?

- What attracted you to this company?

- Why should we hire you?

- What did you like least about your last job?

- When were you most satisfied in your job?

- What can you do for us that other candidates can't?

- What were the responsibilities of your last position?

- Why are you leaving your present job?

- What do you know about this industry?

- What do you know about our company?

- Are you willing to relocate?

- Do you have any questions for me?

Behavioral Interview Questions:

- What was the last project you headed up, and what was its outcome?

- Give me an example of a time that you felt you went above and beyond the call of duty at work.

- Can you describe a time when your work was criticized?

- Have you ever been on a team where someone was not pulling their own weight? How did you handle it?

- Tell me about a time when you had to give someone difficult feedback. How did you handle it?

- What is your greatest failure, and what did you learn from it?

- What irritates you about other people, and how do you deal with it?

- If I were your supervisor and asked you to do something that you disagreed with, what would you do?

- What was the most difficult period in your life, and how did you deal with it?

- Give me an example of a time you did something wrong. How did you handle it?

- What irritates you about other people, and how do you deal with it?

- Tell me about a time where you had to deal with conflict on the job.

- If you were at a business lunch and you ordered a rare steak and they brought it to you well done, what would you do?

- If you found out your company was doing something against the law, like fraud, what would you do?

- What assignment was too difficult for you, and how did you resolve the issue?

- What's the most difficult decision you've made in the last two years and how did you come to that decision?

- Describe how you would handle a situation if you were required to finish multiple tasks by the end of the day, and there was no conceivable way that you could finish them.

- Give an example of an occasion when you used logic to solve a problem.

- Give an example of a goal you reached and tell me how you achieved it.

- Describe a decision you made that was unpopular and how you handled implementing it.

- Have you gone above and beyond the call of duty? If so, how?

- What do you do when your schedule is interrupted? Give an example of how you handle it.

- Have you had to convince a team to work on a project they weren't thrilled about? How did you do it?

- Have you handled a difficult situation with a co-worker? How?

- Tell me about how you worked effectively under pressure.

- Describe a major change that occurred in a job that you held. How did you adapt to this change?

- Tell us about a situation in which you had to adjust to changes over which you had no control. How did you handle it?

- Tell us about a time that you had to adapt to a difficult situation.

- What do you do when priorities change quickly? Give one example of when this happened.

- Describe a project or idea that was implemented primarily because of your efforts. What was your role? What was the outcome?

- Describe a time when you made a suggestion to improve the work in your organization.

- Give an example of an important goal that you set in the past. Tell about your success in reaching it.

- Give two examples of things you've done in previous jobs t hat demonstrate your willingness to work hard.

- How many hours a day do you put into your work? What were your study patterns at school?

- Tell us about a time when you had to go above and beyond the call of duty in order to get a job done.

- Tell us about a time when a job had to be completed and you were able to focus your attention and efforts to get it done.

- Tell us about a time when you were particularly effective on prioritizing tasks and completing a project on schedule.

- Tell us about the last time that you undertook a project that demanded a lot of initiative.

- Tell us how you keep your job knowledge current with the ongoing changes in the industry.

- There are times when we work without close supervision or support to get the job done. Tell us about a time when you found yourself in such a situation and how things turned out. What impact did you have in your last job?

- What is the most competitive work situation you have experienced? How did you handle it? What was the result?

- What is the riskiest decision you have made? What was the situation? What happened?

- What kinds of challenges did you face on your last job? Give an example of how you handled them.

- What projects have you started on your own recently? What prompted you to get started?

- What sorts of things have you done to become better qualified for your career?

- What was the best idea that you came up with in your career? How did you apply it?

- When you disagree with your manager, what do you do? Give an example.

- When you have a lot of work to do, how do you get it all done? Give an example?

- Describe the project or situation which best demonstrates your analytical abilities. What was your role?

- Developing and using a detailed procedure is often very important in a job. Tell about a time when you needed to develop and use a detailed procedure to successfully complete a project.

- Give a specific example of a time when you used good judgment and login in solving a problem.

- Give me a specific example of a time when you used good judgment and logic in solving a problem.

- Give me an example of when you took a risk to achieve a goal. What was the outcome?

- How did you go about making the changes (step by step)? Answer in depth or detail such as "What were you thinking at that point?" or "Tell me more about meeting with that person", or "Lead me through your decision process".

- Relate a specific instance when you found it necessary to be precise in order to complete the job.

- Tell us about a job or setting where great precision to detail was required to complete a task. How did you handle that situation?

- Tell us about a time when you had to analyze information and make a recommendation. What kind of thought process did you go through? What was your reasoning behind your decision?

- Tell us about your experience in past jobs that required you to be especially alert to details while doing the task involved.

- What is your definition of success?
- Do you believe that you are successful?

Salary Questions:

- What salary are you seeking?
- What's your salary history?
- If I were to give you this salary you requested but let you write your job description for the next year, what would it say?

Career Development Questions:

- What are you looking for in terms of career development?
- How do you want to improve yourself in the next year?
- What kind of goals would you have in mind if you got this job?
- If I were to ask your last supervisor to provide you additional training or exposure, what would she suggest?

Getting Started Questions:

- How would you go about establishing your credibility quickly with the team?
- How long will it take for you to make a significant contribution?
- What do you see yourself doing within the first 30 days of this job?
- If selected for this position, can you describe your strategy for the first 90 days?

More About You:

- How would you describe your work style?

- What would be your ideal working situation?

- What do you look for in terms of culture -- structured or entrepreneurial?

- Give examples of ideas you've had or implemented.

- What techniques and tools do you use to keep yourself organized?

- If you had to choose one, would you consider yourself a big-picture person or a detail-oriented person?

- Tell me about your proudest achievement.

- Who was your favorite manager and why?

- What do you think of your previous boss?

- Was there a person in your career who really made a difference?

- What kind of personality do you work best with and why?

- What are you most proud of?

- What do you like to do?

- What are your lifelong dreams?

- What do you ultimately want to become?

- What is your personal mission statement?

- What are three positive things your last boss would say about you?

- What negative thing would your last boss say about you?

- What three character traits would your friends use to describe you?

- What are three positive character traits you don't have?
- If you were interviewing someone for this position, what traits would you look for?
- List five words that describe your character.
- Who has impacted you most in your career and how?
- What is your greatest fear?
- What is your biggest regret and why?
- What's the most important thing you learned in school?
- Why did you choose your major?
- What will you miss about your present/last job?
- What is your greatest achievement outside of work?
- What are the qualities of a good leader? A bad leader?
- Do you think a leader should be feared or liked?
- How do you feel about taking no for an answer?
- How would you feel about working for someone who knows less than you?
- How do you think I rate as an interviewer?
- Tell me one thing about yourself you wouldn't want me to know.
- Tell me the difference between good and exceptional.
- What kind of car do you drive?
- There's no right or wrong answer, but if you could be anywhere in the world right now, where would you be?
- What's the last book you read?
- What magazines do you subscribe to?

- What's the best movie you've seen in the last year?

- What would you do if you won the lottery?

- Who are your heroes?

- What do you like to do for fun?

- What do you do in your spare time?

- What is your favorite memory from childhood?

Interview Questions to Ask

- How would you describe the responsibilities of the position?

- How would you describe a typical week/day in this position?

- Is this a new position? If not, what did the previous employee go on to do?

- What is the company's management style? (Be prepared to specify)

- Who does this position report to? If I am offered the position, can I meet him/her?

- How many people work in this office/department?

- How much travel is expected?

- Is relocation a possibility?

- What is the typical work week? Is overtime expected?

- What are the prospects for growth and advancement?

- Are there any examples?

- What do you like about working here?

- Would you like a list of references?

- If I am extended a job offer, how soon would you like me

to start?

- When can I expect to hear from you?

- Are there any other questions I can answer for you?

- Do you have a training program for this position? If so, please describe it for me.

- Will the responsibilities of this position expand with time and experience on the job?

- What are you looking for in a candidate?

- What is the next step in the interview process?

Interview Questions NOT to Ask

- What does this company do? (Do your research ahead of time!)

- If I get the job when can I take time off for vacation? (Wait until you get the offer to mention prior commitments)

- Can I change my schedule if I get the job? (If you need to figure out the logistics of getting to work don't mention it now...)

- Did I get the job? (Don't be impatient. They'll let you know.)

BIBLIOGRAPHY

Assorgi, Frank, interview by Brian L. Burns Sr. *Community Development Consultant, Friends of Epilepsy* (2009).

Calvin, Ken, interview by Brian L. Burns Sr. *Director of Student Services, College of Business, Chicago State University* (2010).

Deane, Michael. "7 Interview Don'ts." *www.best-job-interview.com.* March 19, 2010.

Doyle, Alison. "Bahavioral Job Interview Question Samples." *www.about.com.*

—. "How To Dress For An Interview." *www.About.com.*

—. "Interview Questions to Ask the Interviewer." *www.About.com.*

—. "Job Interview Questions and Best Answers." *www.About.com.*

—. "Resume Gap, How to Explain an Employment Gap." *www.About.com.*

—. "Top Ten Behavioral Interview Questions." *www.About.com.*

—. "What is a Behavioral Interview and Behavioral Interview Questions and Answers." *www.About.com.*

—. "Winning Interview Skills, A Guide to Successful Interviewing." *www.About.com.*

Georgevich, Don. "Interview Answers For Tough Questions-What To Say If You've Been Fired, Laid Off or Out of Work." *http:// EzineArticles.com/?expert=Don_Georgevich.*

Ivy, Parrish, interview by Brian L. Burns Sr. *Senior Tax Consultant, Deloitte Tax LLP* (2010).

Jacobe, Dennis, Chief Economist . "Gallup Finds U.S. Unemployment Up Slightly in January to 9.8%; Underemployment at 18.9% , compared with 19.0% at end of December." *www.gallup.com/ poll/145922/gallup-finds-unemployment-slightly-January.aspx.* February 3, 2011

Joyce, Erin. "6 Career-Killing Facebook Mistakes." *Investopedia.com.* April 6, 2010.

Levitt, Julie Griffin. *Your Career: How To Make It Happen, 5th Ed.* Boise: South Western Publications, 2004.

Lorenz, Kate. "The Best Questions to Ask in the Interview." *www. Careerbuilder.com.*

Mahdi, Abdul, interview by Brian L. Burns Sr. *Assisatnat Director of Career Development Center, Chicago State University* (2010).

Perkins, Judi. "Fired? The Interview Solution." *www.Best-Interview-Strategies.com.*

Peterson, Thad. "100 Potential Interview Questions." *www.monster.com.*

Reh, F. John. "Job Interview Questions to Ask." *www.About.com.*

Rudloff, Alex. "Complete List of Behavioral Interview Questions." *Interviewing*, May 21, 2007.

Staff Writer. "What To Bring To A Job Interview-Interview Basics." *http://www.articlesbase.com.* May 19, 2008.

—. "What to Bring to the Interview-What Not to Bring." *http://careers.stateuniversity.com.*

Staff Writers. "35 Things To Avoid At Your Job Interview." *www.businessschool.com.*

—. "Answer Difficult Interview Questions about Salary." *www.best-job-interview.com.*

—. "Answering Strange Interview Questions." *www.best-job-interview.com.*

—. "How To Explain Being Fired or Laid Off In A Job Interview." *www.Monster.com.* April 29, 2010.

—. "Job Interview Answers To Tough Interview Questions." *www.best-job-interview.com.*

—. "Prepare For The Behavioral Interview." *www.best-job-interview. com.*

—. "Questions to Ask Employers During Interviews." *www.vt.edu/ studentaffairs.*

Statistics,Bureau of Labor. "Unemployment Rises Slightly to 9.0% in April." www.ncsl.org. May 6, 2011

Statistics, U.S Bureau of Labor. "U.S. Payroll Rises 244K in April; Unemployment Rate 9.0%." www.tradingeconomics.com/Unite-States/Unemployment-Rate. May 7, 2011

Thompson, Robin. "What Should One Bring To An Interview." *www. essortment.com.*

TIPS TO HAVE A COMPETITIVE ADVANTAGE IN A JOB INTERVIEW.

The job market is very competitive. In order to have a competitive advantage of getting that job, you must have the inside scoop of doing well on an interview. There are several things that hiring managers look for in qualified candidates to add to their teams. There are some very important factors for a successful interview such as personal appearance, time management, the ability to effectively answer and ask questions and verbal and non-verbal communication. This guide will help you with the skills and knowledge you need to know in order to nail that interview. This is a comprehensive but simple to understand guide for the kid trying to obtain his first summer job, the college student entering the work force for the first time to the seasoned veteran trying to get back into the workforce after many years.

www.ingramcontent.com/pod-product-compliance
Lightning Source LLC
Chambersburg PA
CBHW030415290526
45785CB00004B/2001